Pebble Plus

LET'S LOOK AT COUNTRIES

LET'S LOOK AT
JAPAN

BY A. M. REYNOLDS

raintree
a Capstone company — publishers for children

Raintree is an imprint of Capstone Global Library Limited, a company incorporated in England and Wales having its registered office at 264 Banbury Road, Oxford, OX2 7DY – Registered company number: 6695582

www.raintree.co.uk
myorders@raintree.co.uk

Edited by Erika L Shores
Designed by Juliette Peters
Picture research by Jo Miller
Production by Kathy McColley
Originated by Capstone Global Library Ltd
Printed and bound in India

ISBN 978 1 4747 6944 0
23 22 21 20 19
10 9 8 7 6 5 4 3 2 1

British Library Cataloguing in Publication Data
A full catalogue record for this book is available from the British Library.

Acknowledgements
We would like to thank the following for permission to reproduce photographs: Getty Images: kokouu, 17; Newscom: Pictures From History/William Ng, 10; Shutterstock: 501room, 15, anuar.mohammad, 21, Blue Planet Studio, Cover Top, cowardlion, 14, f11photo, 5, Globe Turner, 22 (Inset), gontabunta, 13, KPG Payless2, Cover Middle, Martin Voeller, 8, nate, 4, panparinda, 9, Perati Komson, 11, Sean Pavone, 1, 3, shikema, 22-23, 24, Shuttertong, Cover Bottom, Cover Back, tororo reaction, 7, Vincent St. Thomas, 19.

CONTENTS

Where is Japan?

Japan is an island country in eastern Asia. It is nearly twice the size of the UK. Japan's capital is Tokyo.

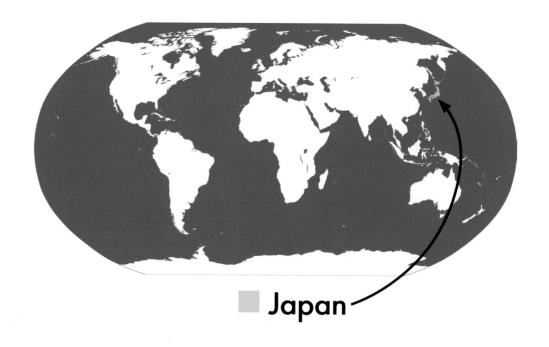

Japan

Tokyo, Japan

From mountains to the seas

The Pacific Ocean circles Japan.

Japan has four main islands.

It also has more than 6,800 smaller

islands. Mountains and forests cover

much of the land.

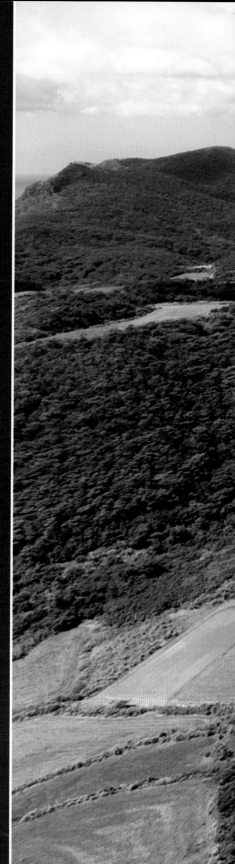

In the wild

Bears and deer live in Japan's forests. Monkeys and flying squirrels climb the trees. Japanese giant salamanders swim in streams.

giant salamander

snow monkeys

People

People have lived in Japan for more than 10,000 years. Most people live in cities on the coast. Japan has a leader called an emperor.

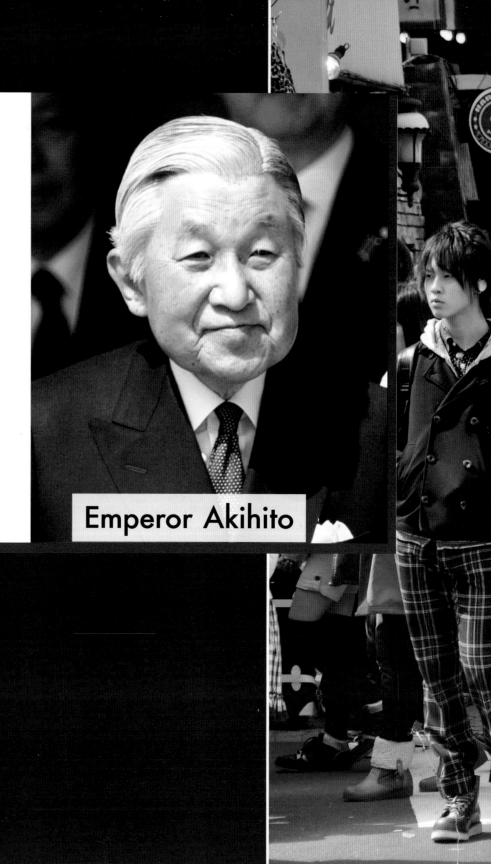

Emperor Akihito

11

At the table

Traditional Japanese foods are healthy. These foods include fish, rice and vegetables. Sushi and rice crackers are some Japanese snack foods.

Festivals

Japan celebrates spring with the Cherry Blossom Festival. People meet their friends and picnic under the trees. They enjoy the cherry blossoms.

At work

There are lots of types of jobs in Japan.
Many Japanese people work in shops,
banks and offices. Some people make cars
and electronics in factories. Other Japanese
people work in farming and fishing.

Transport

People in Japan travel by car, bus, bike, train and plane. Trains travel all over Japan. People travel in very fast trains called bullet trains.

Famous place

Visitors come to Japan to see Mount Fuji. Some people climb 3,766 metres (12,389 feet) to the top. It is an active volcano.

QUICK JAPAN FACTS

Japanese flag

Name: Japan
Capital: Tokyo
Other major cities: Osaka, Nagoya and Sapporo
Population: 126,451,398 (2017 estimate)
Size: 377,915 sq km (145,914 square miles)
Language: Japanese
Money: Japanese Yen

GLOSSARY

active volcano currently erupting or likely to erupt

capital city or town in a country where the government is based

emperor male leader who is the symbol of the country's customs and beliefs

flying squirrel type of squirrel that can glide between branches of trees

giant salamander second largest amphibian in the world

sushi small rice roll wrapped in nori (seaweed)

traditional relating to ideas, ways and beliefs that are passed down from one generation to the next

FIND OUT MORE

BOOKS

Children's Illustrated Atlas (DK Children's Atlas), Andrew Brooks (DK Children, 2016)

Japan (A Benjamin Blog and His Inquisitive Dog Guide), Anita Ganeri (Raintree, 2014)

Japan (Info Buzz), Izzi Howell (Franklin Watts, 2018)

WEBSITES

www.bbc.co.uk/programmes/p011n9fv
Learn a Japanese style of drumming.

www.dkfindout.com/uk/earth/continents/asia
Find out more about Asia.

COMPREHENSION QUESTIONS

1. What is the capital of Japan?

2. Describe some of Japan's traditional foods.

3. Which season does the Cherry Blossom Festival celebrate?

INDEX